Six Attitudes for Winners

NORMAN VINCENT PEALE

POCKET GUIDES™
Tyndale House Publishers, Inc.
Wheaton, Illinois

All Scripture in this book is from *The Holy Bible,* King James Version, unless otherwise noted.

Six Attitudes for Winners is adapted from:

You Can Overcome Any Problem © 1971 by Norman Vincent Peale

Overcoming Anxiety and Fear © 1967 by Norman Vincent Peale

Enthusiasm! The Action Handbook © 1973 by Norman Vincent Peale

Stop Worrying and Start Living © 1982 by Foundation for Christian Living

The Power to Change Your Life © 1972 by Norman Vincent Peale

You've Got a Future! An Action Manual © 1974 by Norman Vincent Peale

Help Yourself . . . with God's Help © 1976 by Foundation for Christian Living

The above booklets were published by Foundation for Christian Living, Pawling, N.Y.

Pocket Guide is a trademark of Tyndale House Publishers, Inc.
Library of Congress Catalog Card Number 87-50032
ISBN 0-8423-5906-0
Copyright©1989 by Norman Vincent Peale
Printed in the United States of America

97   96   95   94

12   11   10   9

CONTENTS

Positive: No Problem Is Too Great to Solve

J. C. Penney, a longtime friend of mine, was a vigorous ninety-five years old when we were seated together at a speaker's table in New York's Hotel Waldorf-Astoria. We fell to discussing problems and what to do about them. "You have had plenty of difficulty in your long lifetime, J. C.," I said. "What is your philosophy of a problem?"

His answer was characteristic of this great and good man. "Well, Norman," he replied, "actually I'm grateful for all my problems. As each of them was overcome I became stronger and more able to meet those yet to come. I grew on my difficulties."

Like J. C. Penney, at the very beginning of your effort to overcome your problems you will need to take a positive mental attitude toward them.

HOW DO YOU LOOK AT FACTS?
In my office is a sign someone made for me. It reads, "Attitudes are more important than

facts." That legend has helped me handle my own problems because it teaches how to look at a fact. The negativist may say, "Here is a hard, tough fact. You just can't get around it. A fact is a fact and that is that."

But the positivist, on the other hand, says, "Yes, here is a fact. But there is a way to deal with this or any fact: Go around it or under it or over it or hit it straight on. A problem is for solving and I've got what it takes to do just that."

The negativist is likely to be defeated by the fact, while the positivist will probably handle it creatively. It is not so much the fact as your attitude toward the fact that determines the outcome.

THE TERRITORY NOBODY WANTED

Consider the case of two salesmen. One was assigned territory that had produced very little business for the company. This territory had the reputation that "nobody can do anything with it."

The man went to his new territory in full acceptance of the general appraisal that there was no business possibility there. "So," he reasoned, "why knock myself out? I am being unfairly treated by having this nonproducing area hung around my neck."

You will not be surprised to know that he failed to develop any appreciable amount of new business and left the company. He never even gave it a try. It was for him a fact that no opportunity was available there. His attitude toward it was negative. Results? Negative!

A second salesman, brought in from across the country, knew nothing about the territory except that it was centered around a thriving metropolitan community. No one had told him that it contained no sales possibility, so he proceeded to get busy and made many sales.

"Why, this is an unworked gold mine!" he exclaimed. All his thinking was positive and his activity was positive. He made a great success of the territory. But so profound was this man's positive mental attitude that had anyone told him it was a bad territory he wouldn't have believed it. And why should he? There were hundreds of thousands of people living there and they needed his product and he was there to see they had it. He was a successful man.

THREE STEPS TO A POSITIVE MENTAL ATTITUDE

1. *Think, don't react.* When a difficulty strikes, the tendency is to panic or to be upset, even to be resentful. Such reactions are emotionally conditioned, and if one's acts are determined in such a state of mind they are likely to lack full rationality.

One must discipline himself to be calm in his thinking. He must cool it. For the mind cannot think when it is hot; only when the mind is cool will it produce those rational, factual concepts that lead to solutions. So do not allow yourself to emote. Think!

Actually, your head is your greatest asset. Keep it always under disciplinary control. Remember the statement credited to Thomas A. Edison: "The chief purpose of the body is to carry the brain around." The great inventor knew that it is in the mind, working in non-overheated fashion, that we get ideas, not impulses. And with these sound ideas we solve problems.

2. *Become a* how *thinker.* After thirty years of hard work Fred lost his business because of a crooked partner. I expected him to be full of bitterness when he came to see me. Instead, he told me he had found his assets to be much greater than his liabilities.

"All I had when I began thirty years ago was $50. Now I have $500. So you see, I'm ahead on that," he said with a grin. "I started with a wonderful wife, and I still have her, thank God. And I'm way ahead on experience."

Within a year after this setback he had started another business and was doing well. But the statement he made that really stayed with me was this: "I decided I would not be an *if* thinker, but a *how* thinker."

That's quite a thought-provoking distinction. The *if* thinker broods over a difficulty or a setback, saying bitterly to himself, "If only I had done thus and so. . . . If only this or that circumstance had been different. . . . If others had not treated me so unfairly. . . ." So it goes from explanation to explanation, round and round, getting nowhere. The world is full of defeated *if* thinkers.

"Every problem contains the seeds of its own solution."—Stanley Arnold

---

The *how* thinker, on the other hand, wastes no energy on post-mortems when trouble or even disaster hits him. He immediately starts looking for the best solution, for he knows there always is a solution. He asks himself, "How can I use this setback creatively? How can I work something good out of it?"

The *how* thinker gets problems solved effectively because he knows that values are always inherent in difficulty. He wastes no time with futile *ifs* but goes right to work on the creative *hows*.

3. *Believe you can and you can.* This dynamic principle has been demonstrated in the lives of too many believers to leave any doubt concerning its validity. It is very important to believe that you can, with God's help, meet and overcome all problems. The words *believe* and *can* are linked together in a creative action unity. If you believe you can, you can.

A man who had been experiencing one failure after another saw in a book a phrase that gripped him. It was this: "Expect the best and get it." It hit him hard and he admitted to himself that he had been thinking defeating thoughts. Every day he had been expecting the worst and usually getting it.

So he began searching through the Bible for "practical" ideas that would erase his failure image. He found many, including these two: "Ask, and it shall be given you; seek, and ye shall find; knock, and it shall be opened unto you" (Matt. 7:7), and "For God hath not given us the spirit of fear; but of power, and of love, and of a sound mind" (2 Tim. 1:7).

These Scriptures did a real mind-washing job on him, cleaning out doubts and inferiorities. "I decided," he said, "to take a different attitude toward my job. I would start out each morning saying, 'I like my job. This is going to be the greatest day of my life.' I began to see that if I did not believe in myself I could not expect anyone else to believe in me." Such was the experience of R. Gene Scalf, who told his story in *Guideposts*.

So start buttressing your weak faith with the powerful concepts of the Bible. The Bible is packed full of faith-producing thoughts that can revamp your mental attitude. When that happens you will become a believer who can believe your way through your problems.

YOUR PROBLEM: PEARL
OF GREAT PRICE
Some years ago I knew an inspirational man who taught me the technique of looking for "the pearl of great price" buried at the heart

of a problem. As a young man burdened by a
seemingly insoluble problem, I went to him
for advice. "So you've got a problem," he
said. "Congratulations!"

"How come congratulations?" I asked in
surprise. Sympathy seemed more in order.
"Because," he replied cheerfully, "out of this
problem some big wonderful thing may come
into your life."

At his encouragement I outlined the problem in full detail. He listened carefully as I
laid out the entire problem before him.
"There it is, this big problem of yours. Let's
not be afraid of it—the face of it is not grim.
Actually it is smiling at you, asking that you
play hide-and-seek with it. There is something great hiding in it. The fun is for you to
find it."

Whimsically he began poking with his forefinger at an imaginary mass laid on the table. "Every problem has a soft spot," he explained. "We'll find it." Presently he chuckled. "Here it is. Now let's start breaking this problem apart. I'm sure we will find something wonderful in it."

And under his skillful guidance we did find one of the greatest values in my personal experience. I have had profound respect for problems ever since, knowing that each one that comes my way may come bearing a priceless gift of know-how, insight, and understanding.

Don't fight a problem. And never complain when a problem strikes you. Instead, start asking questions of the problem. For it is full of know-how for you. Actually, a problem is one of God's greatest methods for teaching you, for helping you to develop.

CUT YOUR PROBLEM DOWN TO SIZE

Our tendency often is to feel inferior and inadequate in the presence of a problem. In the mind one tends to blow the problem out of proportion to its actual size. It scares and frightens, not because it is too big for us, but because our fearful thoughts have invested it with a difficulty it does not really possess.

An important procedure is to cut the problem down to its true proportions; reduce it to size. Empty out the fear-panic-inadequacy feeling and start thinking with objective rationality. Set the problem straight.

In a business office I found a man behind a

desk on which sheets of paper were laid out in an orderly pattern. Each sheet contained handwritten notations. This man said, "You may be curious about what goes on here with these papers. Actually I'm dealing with a pretty rough problem. And I have my own way of doing that."

He went on to tell me there was a time in his life when he was "licked" by problems. Then he met an older businessman who said, "Look, Jack, I've found that usually no problem is as forbidding as it seems. I discovered that if you begin taking a problem apart, breaking it up into its component parts, you can handle the whole problem by dealing with those parts separately. Take a problem in bits and pieces. The matter won't look so big to you."

"That advice made sense," my friend said, "so my method is what you see here. I thoroughly analyze the problem, breaking it up and writing on these papers its various aspects. Then," he continued, "I pray and ask for guidance as to how to proceed.

"Usually I chisel off the easiest part of the problem first and dispose of that. In this manner I continue to work and pray until the problem is reduced to its central core. Then it's wonderful how adequate I feel in dealing with the essence of the matter.

"This method really works," he declared enthusiastically. "So much so that I'm getting a greater kick out of life than ever. I've found that I am bigger than any problem," he concluded stoutly.

SEEK SUPERNATURAL HELP

When we assert that you can overcome any problem, we are taking into account that you do not have to do it entirely on your own. For, you see, you have extra help available from God. You have the advantage of insight and strength greater than any human being possesses. What problem can possibly be too much for God and you acting together in perfect harmony? It's the greatest combination of all.

An attractive young wife glowingly told me of the many ways in which God had been with her in problems. And she had plenty of problems. Among other difficulties, she had been crippled by infantile paralysis. But the victorious spirit so evident within her demonstrated that she knew how to overcome any problem.

"What is your secret?" I asked admiringly.

"Oh," she declared excitedly, "I have God's telephone number. I can call him anytime. And his line is never busy. He always answers."

"And what is God's telephone number?" I asked.

"It's JER. 33:3. That is Jeremiah, chapter 33, verse 3, where it says, 'Call unto me, and I will answer thee, and show thee great and mighty things, which thou knowest not.'"

Certainly you can handle any and all of your problems if you have "God's telephone number," knowing that Divine counsel and help are always readily available.

If problems seem too much for you, perhaps it is because you are not calling upon God. His phone is not disconnected. Nor is the line busy. He is right there waiting to hear from you. Dial his number (JER. 33:3). Call upon him and he will answer you at once. He can show you a way out of your difficulties. He can guide you in overcoming any problem.

Courageous: I Have Nothing to Fear

Any emotion is removable. Anger is removable. Depression is removable. Hatred is removable. Prejudice is removable. Greatest of all, fear is removable.

One of the first steps in overcoming any fear is simply to realize that it is, for a fact, removable. Never entertain the notion that you must live with fear all your life. You need not. Do not imagine that because your mother, father, or grandfather had apprehensive fears that you must have them also. If you are willing to be harassed by fear all your life you can be, very easily. But you do not need to be.

FACING LIFE'S STORMS

Eleanor Roosevelt once said: "You gain strength, courage, and confidence by every experience by which you really stop to look fear in the face."

When a person determinedly stands up to something, that something tends to fold and

> "The first duty for a man is still that of subduing Fear. . . . A man's acts are slavish . . . till he have got Fear under his feet."—Thomas Carlyle

finally give way. There is much less danger in standing up to a difficulty or fear than in trying to avoid or run away from it.

An old cowboy said he had learned life's most important lesson from Hereford cows. All his life he had worked on cattle ranches where winter storms took a heavy toll among the herds. Freezing rains whipped across the prairies. Howling, bitter winds piled snow into enormous drifts. Temperatures might drop quickly to below-zero. Flying ice cut into the flesh. In this maelstrom of nature's violence most cattle would turn their backs to the icy blasts and slowly drift downwind, mile upon mile. Finally, intercepted by a boundary fence, they would pile up against the barrier and die by the scores.

But the Herefords acted differently. Cattle of this breed would instinctively head into the windward end of the range. There they would stand shoulder-to-shoulder facing the storm's blast, heads down against its onslaughts. "You most always found the Herefords alive and well," said the cowboy. "I guess that is the greatest lesson I ever learned on the prairies—just face life's storms."

The lesson is valid. Do not attempt to evade things you fear and go drifting with the wind to keep away from them. Every human being has to decide again and again, and still again, whether to meet fearsome difficulties head-on or to try running away.

Actually, most fears are baseless and empty anyway. A friend of mine figured out that over his lifetime 92 percent of the things he feared never did happen. About 8 percent did happen, and of them he said, "Oh, I just stood up to them, handled them, and overcame them." He added, "All fears are controllable."

THREE-STEP PLAN TO CANCEL YOUR FEARS

1. *Resolve to be a person of faith.* In canceling out fear the number one thing to do is to say determinedly: "I do not want to be motivated by anxiety and fear any more. I want to cast out fear and anxiety from my mind and no longer be dominated by them. I now decide—I now determine—I now will—that my anxiety and fear be brought under control, even eliminated, and that I become a person of faith."

Of course saying these things, however strongly, will not in itself accomplish them; but they will be accomplished when you strongly affirm them and determine to make your desire and decision really stick.

2. *Work on one fear at a time.* Take a piece of paper and list all of the things you are afraid of. Make as complete and as honest

> ## Stonewall Jackson: "Never Take Counsel of Your Fears"
>
> Remember the old story about General Stonewall Jackson? One night during the Civil War Jackson was in conference with his generals. He was planning a daring sortie in the Shenandoah Valley. It was a brilliant plan, strategically. The odds were high, but the possibility of success existed.
>
> At the conclusion of the meeting one of Jackson's generals said, "But, General Jackson, I'm afraid of this. I fear we can't quite carry it off."
>
> Jackson, so the story goes, rose, put his hand on the subordinate's shoulder, and said, "Never take counsel of your fears, General. Never take counsel of your fears."

a listing as possible. Then study your list carefully to determine your most pervasive fear, the one that may be present every day and that disturbs you the most. Decide to attack that particular fear alone.

I suggest this procedure because your strength no doubt is equal to only one fear at a time. Conceivably an attack upon the entire lot of them would be more than you could successfully mount. But if you overcome first a particular fear and then another, and another, presently you will gather strength to defeat your entire fear pattern.

The American Indians believed that the

strength of a scalped warrior passed into the brave who killed him. An Indian brave was strong in proportion to the number of scalps strung around his waist. Scalp your fears one at a time and presently you can take on bigger and stronger fears and overcome each in turn.

3. *Increase your faith.* A third procedure is what might be called a spiritual crash program, or a method for increasing faith quickly. In the best sense faith is, of course, the result of a long-developing spiritual process. But since we have the practical problem of dealing with fear and just haven't the faith to counteract it, we are left with the necessity for building faith up at once.

To do this I suggest taking large "doses" of faith into your mind. Work at it zealously and constantly, with the definite purpose of saturating your very consciousness. Search the Scriptures for passages that express the greatest values people have ever had. Commit these to memory. Say them over and over until they completely dominate your thinking.

It will not be very long until these powerful faith thoughts begin displacing your fears.

END YOUR FEAR OF PEOPLE

When I was a young reporter on the old *Detroit Journal* my editor, Grove Patterson, took a kindly interest in me. He was a man of keen and perceptive insights. One day he called me into his office. "Norman," he said, "I get the feeling that you've got a lot of fear and anxiety. You must get rid of it. What in the world is there to be afraid of? Why should you or I, or anybody, go through life like a scared rabbit? The good Lord has told us that he will help us and be with us."

I shall always remember that conversation. "Look, son," he continued, "I'm going to give you a little advice. The only one in this world to fear is God, and that doesn't mean to be afraid of him. It means to esteem him. There is nothing else to fear. So never be afraid of anything or anybody."

"But, Mr. Patterson," I said, "that's a pretty big order. How can anyone possibly go through life afraid of nothing or nobody?"

He leveled a long, inky finger at me. "Listen," he said, "I'll tell you how. 'Be strong and of a good courage; be not afraid, . . . for the Lord thy God *is* with [you] whithersoever

---

Two Faith Thoughts
- Psalm 34: "I sought the Lord, and he heard me, and delivered me from all my fears." To say that I sought the Lord means that I really determined to find him, and this very determination brought me to him.
- Psalm 23: "I will fear no evil: for thou art with me." Get the presence of God fixed in your mind and fear will fade away.

[you go].'* Just hang onto that promise," he added, "and don't forget that it's made by Someone who never let anybody down."

The world is full of individuals who live miserable lives because fear of other people affects their personal relationships. The employee fears the boss. The diffident person is fearful of assertive types. I have known wives who were afraid of their husbands and vice versa; and nowadays it seems that not a few parents are actually afraid of their children. Some people actually give up participation in an event or group because someone else makes them feel inferior.

How may fear of other people be overcome?

1. *Help other shy people.* Always know that in every group are other shy people. You may be surprised to discover who they are; often the loudest talker, for instance, is covering up his inferiority feelings. Single out a shy person in the group and show him attention. This will help him, and it will help you doubly.

2. *Be yourself entirely.* Remind yourself that you are distinctive, that in fact you are the only one of *you* in existence. This will free you from a slavish simulation of other people. The effort to be like someone else is in essence a fear of other people, or the fear of being different.

3. *Love others.* The top curative factor in overcoming fear of other people is to learn to love them. "Perfect love casts out fear"

*Joshua 1:9

(1 John 4:18). The more you develop genuine appreciation and esteem for others, the less you will feel inferior in their presence and the easier, more normal, your relationships with them will be.

4. *Pray for people* with whom you feel backward or uncomfortable. Ask God to help them with their problems—they have some, also, you know. In time they will sense your prayerful regard and appreciate you for it.

END YOUR FEAR OF FAILURE

More people than might be supposed are deeply troubled by the fear of failure. It is a dangerous fear to have working against you, for it can cause the personality to freeze and therefore induce the very failure you fear.

Everyone is bound to fail at times and the important question is, how do you react to failure? Actually a failure can be an excellent teacher—we can learn from our mistakes how not to do a thing. Then, too, we can learn from our successes how a thing is done right. It is important to seek persistently within both failure and success to discover new insights and know-hows. You can bring great accomplishments out of what at first seemed overwhelming failure; but if you permit failure to continue as failure, it will be failure in outcome forever.

So when you experience a failure, take a perceptive look at it, ask yourself why you failed, then go back at it again wiser, more competent, and never in any sense entertain-

Love Overcomes Fear

A young man consulted me about his fear of his boss, a stern man with whom few ever got close. The young man said, "I almost shake outwardly when I am called to his office, and my job requires my reporting daily to him." I offered the opinion that the boss may have become seemingly stern and hard due to some personal inward problems of loneliness or trouble. I suggested that the young man pray for the employer and send out thoughts of friendly affection toward him. "It will be like trying to dent a wall of steel," he complained.

But as it turned out, the older man was not as hard as his self-defenses seemed to indicate. When the younger employee changed his attitude to one of regard for the boss as a human being, a warm feeling developed between them, and gradually fear of the employer passed away. It is such a simple law of human relationships: Genuine love and friendliness overcome the fear of other people.

Complete freedom from the fear of other people results when you override your own self-consciousness and become fully aware of other people's needs.

ing the thought that you will continue to fail. Such practice strengthens you in the process of thinking failure out and thinking success in.

There is no satisfaction in this world quite

like overcoming the fear of failure. If you prepare for a frontal assault by planning, learning, thinking, studying, working, believing, and praying, you will have all the ingredients you need to conquer the plaguing fear of failure.

THE SECRET OF COURAGE

The secret of courage is simply and honestly to admit your feelings of failure—then with God's help go on and do your job in spite of them. This procedure will keep fear under control.

Maurice Chevalier was the greatest entertainer of his era. In mid-career, suddenly one night before going onstage he felt extremely dizzy. His brain seemed on fire. Cues seemed to reach him from far away. He tried desperately to get back on the track, but his mind was a jumble. He felt hopelessly lost.

His fellow actors covered up for him that night and for several weeks; but the old debonair ease which was his trademark was gone. He would hesitate, stammer. Failure for the first time in his professional life had come to the great performer.

Ordered to rest, Maurice Chevalier came under the care of Dr. Robert Dubois in the southern part of France. "I'm a beaten man. I'm afraid of being a failure. There is no future for me now," he told the doctor. He was advised to take long walks to repair his damaged nervous system. Yet the inner turmoil did not leave him. He had lost all confidence and he was afraid, afraid.

After a time the doctor suggested he entertain before a small group in the village hall. "But," said Maurice, "I am terrified at the thought. What guarantee is there that my mind will not go blank?" "There are no guarantees," the doctor said slowly. "But you must not be afraid of failing. You are afraid to step on a stage again and so you tell yourself that you're finished. But fear is never a reason for quitting: It is only an excuse. When a brave man encounters fear he admits it, and goes on despite it."

Maurice suffered untold agony of fear before his return appearance in that little town, but he went on and performed very well. Joy welled up inside him. "I knew that I had not conquered fear. I had simply admitted it and gone on despite it; and the scheme worked."

From that night Maurice Chevalier performed before audiences everywhere. "There have been many moments of fear," he said. "The gentle doctor was right; there are no guarantees. But being frightened has never since made me want to quit." And Maurice added: "My own experience has taught me this. If you wait for the perfect moment when all is safe and assured, it may never arrive. Mountains will not be climbed, races won, or lasting happiness achieved."

So don't be afraid to be afraid. Honestly admit your fear and then act as though you were unafraid—and with the help of God go on and do your job with total neglect of fear.

Enthusiastic: Life Is Exciting!

Emerson wrote: "Nothing great was ever achieved without enthusiasm."

There is an extraordinary, dynamic quality about enthusiasm. It is permeated by a victorious attitude so powerful that it sweeps all before it. It brings the personality alive, releasing dormant powers.

The difference between enthusiasm and faith is very slight indeed. Perhaps enthusiasm may be defined as faith that has been set afire. Enthusiasm is one of God's greatest gifts.

"None are so old as those who have outlived enthusiasm."—Henry David Thoreau

---

What is the outstanding characteristic of a little child? It is enthusiasm! He thinks the world is terrific; he just loves it. Everything fascinates him. Huxley said that the secret of genius is to carry the spirit of the child into old age, which means never losing your enthusiasm. But all too few persons retain this excitement, and one reason is that they let enthusiasm be drained off. If you are not getting as much from life as you want to, then examine the state of your enthusiasm.

THROUGH THE EYES OF ENTHUSIASM

My own mother was one of the most enthusiastic persons I ever knew. She got an enormous thrill out of the most ordinary events. She had the ability to see romance and glory in everything.

I recall one foggy night when she and I were crossing from New Jersey to New York City on a ferry boat. To me, there was nothing particularly beautiful about fog seen from a ferry boat, but my mother exclaimed, "Isn't this thrilling?"

"What is thrilling?" I asked.

"Why," she said, "the fog, the lights, that other ferry boat we just passed! Look at the mysterious way its lights fade into the mist."

Just then we heard the sound of a foghorn, deep-throated in the heavy, padded whiteness of the mist. My mother's face was that of an excited child. I had felt nothing about this ride except that I was in a hurry to get across the river.

She stood at the rail that night and eyed me appraisingly. "Norman," she said gently, "I have been giving you advice all your life. Some of it you have taken; some you haven't.

But here is some I want you to take. Make up your mind, right now, that the world is a-thrill with beauty and excitement. Keep yourself sensitized to it. Love the world, its beauty, and its people." Anybody trying consistently to follow that simple course will be blessed with abundant enthusiasm and have a life full of joy.

"MISS NOBODY"

One night I met "Miss Nobody." After a speech in a West Coast city a young woman gave me a limp handshake and said in a small, timid voice, "I thought I'd like to shake hands with you, but I really shouldn't be bothering you. There are so many important people here and I'm just a nobody."

"Please remain. I'd like to talk with you." Later I said, "Now, Miss Nobody, let's have a little visit."

"What did you call me?" she asked in surprise.

"I called you by the only name you gave. You told me you were a Nobody. Have you another name?"

"Of course," she said. "You see, I have quite an inferiority complex. I came to hear you hoping you might say something that would help me."

"Well," I answered, "I'm saying it to you now: You are a child of God." And I advised her to draw herself up tall each day and say to herself, "I am a child of God." I outlined for her some of the techniques in this book for practicing enthusiasm and self-confidence.

Recently, speaking in the same area, an attractive young woman approached. "Do you remember me? I'm the former Miss Nobody." Her enthusiastic manner and the sparkle in her eyes showed her change.

This incident underscores an important fact. You can change! Anybody can change! And even from a dull nobody to an enthusiastic somebody.

HOW TO DEVELOP ENTHUSIASM

1. *Start the day right.* You can condition a day in the first five minutes after you wake up. Henry Thoreau used to lie abed in the morning telling himself all the good news he could think of. Then he arose to meet the day in a world filled with good things, good people, good opportunities.

The late William H. Danforth, a prominent business leader, said, "Every morning pull yourself up to your full height and stand tall. Then think tall—think great, elevated thoughts. Then go out and act tall. Do that and joy will flow to you."

Go on spreading enthusiasm all day, and at night you will have a deposit of joy in your life such as you never had before.

2. *Read your Bible,* for it is full of enthusiasm generators. What greater motivators, for example, are there than: "All things are possible to him that believeth" (Mark 9:23) and "Whatsoever ye shall ask in prayer, believing, ye shall receive" (Matt. 21:22)?

The Bible positively glows with excitement and enthusiasm. "Be renewed," it says in Ephesians 4:23, "in the spirit of your mind," not merely on the surface of your mind, but in the deep spirit that activates your thoughts. Saturate your mind with great passages from the Bible. Then pray to God for guidance and get going!

Two Faith Boosters
- Every morning and every evening of your life articulate these words: "I can do all things through Christ who strengthens me" (Phil. 4:13, NKJV).
- Every day three times say: "This is the day which the Lord has made. We will rejoice and be glad in it" (Psalm 118:24, NKJV).

---

3. *Love life and people.* Love people. Love the sky, love beauty, love God. The person who loves always becomes enthusiastic. Begin today to cultivate the love of living. Like Fred, for example, who runs a little eating place.

Resting a big hand on the counter, he asked me, "OK, brother, what'll you have?"

"Are you Fred?"

"Yep."

"They tell me you have good hamburgers."

"Brother, you never ate such hamburgers."

"OK, let me have one."

Along the counter was an old man who

looked extremely miserable. He was sitting hunched over. His hand shook. After Fred had put my hamburger in front of me he went over and put his hand on that of this old fellow. "That's all right, Bill," he said. "That's all right. I'm going to fix you a bowl of that nice hot soup that you like." Bill nodded gratefully.

Another old man got up and shuffled over to pay his check. Fred said, "Mr. Brown, watch out for the cars out there on the avenue. They come pretty fast at night." And he added, "Have a look at the moonlight on the river. It's mighty pretty tonight."

When I paid my check I couldn't help remarking, "You know something, my friend? I like the way you spoke to those old men. You made them feel that life is good."

"Why not?" he asked. "Life *is* good. Me, I get a kick out of living. They're pretty sad old guys and our place is sort of like home to them. Anyway, I kind of like 'em."

Find needs and fill them. And bring bona fide enthusiasm to your life!

"The worst bankrupt is the man who has lost his enthusiasm. Let a man lose everything in the world but his enthusiasm and he will come through again to success."—H. W. Arnold

4. *Guard your energy level.* To keep full of enthusiasm, as God intended you to be, keep

your intake of energy greater than the outgo of energy. If you are tense and uptight, the constant tension depletes you so that energy dissipates and with it your enthusiasm.

Therefore, discover the great technique of being able to "let go and let God." Ask God for wisdom and guidance, and then give life the very best. Having done your best, leave the outcome to the Lord, trusting in his providence. You will find renewal, new energy, new enthusiasm.

LET ENTHUSIASM TAKE HOLD!

I knew Vince Lombardi, fabulous football coach. When he came to Green Bay he faced a defeated, dispirited team. He stood before them, looked them over silently for a long time, and then in a quiet but intense way said, "Gentlemen, we are going to have a great football team. We are going to win games. Get that. You are going to learn to block. You are going to learn to run. You are going to learn to tackle. You are going to outplay the teams that come against you. Get that.

"And how is this to be done?" he continued. "You are to have confidence in me and enthusiasm for my system. The secret of the whole matter will be what goes on up here. [And he tapped his temple.] Hereafter, I want you to think of only three things: your home, your religion, and the Green Bay Packers, in that order! Let enthusiasm take hold of you!"

The men sat up straight in their chairs. "I

W. Clement Stone: The Power of ". . . Self-Motivators"

W. Clement Stone is a genuinely enthusiastic person. I asked him the secret of his enthusiasm.

"As you know," he answered, "the emotions are not always immediately subject to reason, but they are always immediately subject to action (mental or physical). Furthermore, repetition of the same thought or physical action develops into a habit which, repeated frequently enough, becomes an automatic reflex.

"And that's why I use self-motivators. A self-motivator is an affirmation that you deliberately use to move yourself to desirable action. You repeat a verbal self-motivator fifty times in the morning . . . fifty times at night . . . for a week or ten days, to imprint the words indelibly in your memory."

Some self-motivators are:

- *God is always a good God!*
- *You have a problem . . . that's good!*
- *Within every adversity there is a seed of an equivalent or greater benefit.*
- *Find one good idea that will work and . . . work that one idea!*
- *Do it now!*
- *To be enthusiastic . . . ACT . . . enthusiastically!*

walked out of that meeting," writes the quarterback, "feeling ten feet tall!" That year they won seven games—with virtually the same players who had lost ten games the year before. The next year they won a Division title and the third year the World Championship. Why? Because, added to hard work and skill and love of the sport, enthusiasm made the difference.

What happened to the Green Bay Packers can happen to a church, to a business, to a country, to an individual. What goes on in the mind is what determines outcome. When an individual really gets enthusiasm you can see it in the flash of his eyes, in his alert and vibrant personality. You observe it in the spring of his step. You can see it in the verve of his whole being. Enthusiasm makes the difference in his attitude toward other people, toward his job, toward the world. It makes a great big difference in the zest and delight of human existence.

Are you alive? Are you enthusiastic?

HE LEARNED TO PRACTICE ENTHUSIASM

Suppose life has dealt harshly with you, and the zest, eagerness, thrill, and enthusiasm have gone out of you. How do you recover them? By one of the greatest devices God ever made—rebirth.

Down south one time I had dinner with a group of twenty men, ten ministers and ten laymen. One man in particular was a master storyteller. I remarked to the minister sitting next to me, "This character really has something."

"He surely has," the minister replied. "He's a member of my church. And he's my Exhibit A."

"What do you mean, 'Exhibit A'?"

"You should have seen him a few years ago. He was so gripey and crabbed, people avoided him. He had pains around the heart, he had pains up the arm, he was short of breath. He was a hypochondriac. And he haunted doctors' offices one after another. He took more pills than anybody in town. But they didn't seem to help him. He had built up a splendid business. Yet he was never happy.

"Finally a doctor shipped him off to a specialist in Chicago. And this Chicago specialist was a wise man. He told our friend, 'These pains of yours are pseudo-pains. They do not come from any physical origin; they are induced by wrong, unhealthy thinking. Get your thinking changed, start living a vital enthusiastic life—and you'll be well. That is my prescription. Fifteen hundred dollars, please.'

"Our friend exclaimed, 'Fifteen hundred bucks! For what?'"

"'For knowing what to tell you. You charge plenty in your business. So do I.'" (The doctor later explained he knew this man wouldn't value advice unless he had to pay for it.)

So this maladjusted man returned home and went immediately to his minister, saying, "That doctor in Chicago told me to get my thinking straightened out. You know, that fellow is a highwayman! He charged me fifteen hundred dollars! So how do I get my thinking straightened out? I'll get my fifteen hundred dollars' worth if it kills me!" (Which is precisely what the doctor had foreseen.)

The minister said, "OK, Jim, how far do you live from here? Five miles? I see your chauffeur sitting out there in your car. Call him and dismiss him. I want you to walk home. And as you walk thank God for those feet of yours, thank God for your legs, thank God that you went to Chicago and were told you have a sound body. Walk home practicing enthusiasm for life, for yourself, for the pine forest you pass on the way, for all your friends, for your church, for God. And tomorrow, I want you to walk back here and tell me how you feel."

Eventually the man got wise and asked the minister to walk with him. The minister walked with him all in all a good twenty-five miles, until one day he challenged the man, "Why don't you let go and let the Lord Jesus Christ take over?" And he did.

"That is your storyteller," the minister told me in conclusion. "Exhibit A. He learned to practice enthusiasm and he is a well man—a happy man."

CHAPTER 4

Peaceful: I Don't Need to Worry

Your physical mechanism is sensitive to whatever goes on in your mind. And since worry is located in your mind, it can have a devastating effect on all parts of your body. This is how it works.

A worry thought first cuts a thin trickle or rivulet across the consciousness. Repeated, it deepens into a channel of fear or anxiety. Presently almost every thought comes up tinctured with worry. As a result, you become a person of fear, a confirmed worrier. You have, by this process, created a mental climate in which worry thrives and grows and finally takes over, dominating your whole life experience.

To arrest this tragic process, the first step is to revamp your worry-conditioned mental climate by gradually substituting a spiritual climate. This can be done by inserting into your consciousness a fresh new system of thinking.

The physician's prescription uses the symbol *Rx*, "Take thou." So we suggest, "Take thou" the great Word of God into your mind. Let it dissolve deeply into your conscious control center where your life pattern is formed. It will, if tenaciously held there, drive from your thoughts the infections that have for so long fed the disease of worry.

RX: SEVEN-WEEK HEALING TREATMENT FOR WORRY

Next Sunday begin a seven-week treatment for worry. Insert into your mind powerful healing verses from the Bible, the greatest of all books on mental health.

For instance, on Sunday commit the verse for that week to memory. On Monday, repeat the verse as many times as a worry thought asserts itself. Do the same on Tuesday through Saturday. Then the next Sunday take the second verse suggested and repeat the process.

All through this time, and certainly by the end of the seventh week, the verses will have so firmly affected your mental and spiritual condition that the pervasive healing process will have started. If resolutely continued, a complete healing from the crippling disease of worry will take place and you can really start living a new worry-free life.

Week 1: This coming Sunday begin the treatment by taking into your mind as this week's healing thought Philippians 4:13: "I can do all things through Christ who strengthens me." Repeat it many times each day all week long, and especially whenever worry threatens.

Week 2: The second Sunday and all that week "take" Isaiah 26:3: "Thou wilt keep him in perfect peace, whose mind is stayed on thee: because he trusteth in thee." Say it aloud over and over until it sinks into consciousness. It will produce a peace in which worry cannot live.

Week 3: This Sunday and during the ensuing week memorize Psalm 23:4: "I will fear no evil: for thou art with me." Emphasize by repetition this powerful thought of God's presence and do so many times daily all week long. Worry cannot exist in the same mind in which God is present. Fill your mind full of God.

Week 4: Every day of the week "take" Luke 11:9: "And I say unto you, Ask, and it shall be given you; seek, and ye shall find; knock, and it shall be opened unto you." Again, repeat the text as often as possible, thus driving its healing message deeper and deeper into your mind.

Week 5: On the fifth Sunday and all that following week memorize John 15:7: "If ye abide in me, and my words abide in you, ye shall ask what ye will, and it shall be done unto you." The concept "abide" is important, signifying permanent occupancy. When God lives continuously in your mind, worry cannot exist there for God and worry are incompatible. One of them must go—and it certainly won't be God.

A Prayer When You're Worried

Dear Lord, I'm worried and full of fear. Anxiety and apprehension fill my mind. Could it be that my love for you is weak and imperfect and as a result I am plagued by worry?

I have tried to reassure myself that there is nothing to worry about. But such reassurances do not seem to help. I know that I should just rest myself confidently upon your loving care and guidance. But I have been too nervous even to do that.

Touch me, dear Lord, with your peace and help my disturbed mind to know that you are God and that I need fear no evil. In Christ's name I offer this prayer. Amen.

Week 6: The week of the sixth Sunday, take into your thoughts Mark 11:24: "What things soever ye desire, when ye pray, believe that ye receive them, and ye shall have them."

Week 7: And in the last week, the Rx for spiritual healing is 1 Peter 5:7: "Casting all your care upon him; for he careth for you." This verse means that God loves you and will shoulder all that you have been worrying about. Repeat the words of this text until they lodge well-fixed forever in your thoughts to recondition your entire mental attitude.

Be consistent and habitual in applying the foregoing spiritual prescription for seven weeks and you will be amazed at the progress you will make in eliminating the debilitation of mind and spirit caused by former worry attitudes.

CONVERSION FREED HIM FROM WORRY

A New York City banker, a skeptic and nonbeliever, came to church one Sunday. He had seen our advertisement in the Saturday newspaper stating the next day's sermon topic: "You Can Get Rid of Worry."

He sneered at this in his supposedly sophisticated manner, but the idea, as he put it, "grabbed him and wouldn't let go." So on Sunday there he sat in church, "in the seat of the scornful."

But he was driven by a profound need. His former actions and manner of thinking had all but destroyed his happiness. And they were also endangering his position in business, for his tense and nervous condition was undermining his ability to perform.

He came to God's house as a patient into a doctor's office. And the Great Physician reached him and changed him right there in that pew. He couldn't believe what happened. Later he told me, "I can't explain it, but that church was so packed full of love and faith that I could not withstand it. Suddenly Jesus was by my side. He seemed to say, 'Come unto me and I will give you rest.' I knew

Jesus as a child, but had long since lost him. That Sunday he took me back. What do you know about that?" he concluded.

He went from that life-changing experience in church to his home. "I was astonished at how clear, and even strong, my mind was. I felt a cool, calm sense of power. It was a glorious feeling. I hadn't felt like that in months," he declared.

Then he started writing his worries, old and new, on slips of paper. He studied each one with merciless criticism. A feeling of disgust came over him as he realized that most of the things he had worried about had never happened. Others, that did have some reality, he now knew that he could handle.

With a sweeping gesture, he gathered all those papers representing needless worries into a ball and threw it into a waste receptacle. "Thank you, dear Lord, for your amazing power to change a person, even me. For I am different. I feel it—I know it."

Then he looked at the few slips remaining that represented, he told me, real concerns about which he previously would have had emotional stress. Now he said, "The Lord and I together can take care of these matters."

As he spoke, I took from my shirt pocket a card which I carry with me always and read it to him.

"Lord, help me to remember that nothing is going to happen to me today that you and I together can't handle."

"That's for me," he said. And, enthusiastically, he copied that statement of faith. "I'll carry it in my pocket and in my thoughts too," he added.

In this case, spiritual conversion swept worry away from this man's life. When he refound the Lord, he refound life. He stopped worrying and started living, really living. He is now in charge of himself because the Lord is in charge of him. Christ's redemptive work can create, in any person's thinking, a new climate in which worry withers and dies.

ADDING UP YOUR BLESSINGS TO SUBTRACT YOUR WORRIES

A gospel hymn that was popular some years ago made a lot of sense: "Count your blessings, name them one by one." That song was absolutely sound, both spiritually and psychologically. As you add up your blessings and keep on counting them, your worries will finally get the message that the game is up and will begin fading away.

A man from an upstate city who reads the material put out by the Foundation for Christian Living telephoned saying he desperately needed help. "Everything is going badly," he said, "and I'm worried sick."

"Could just be," I responded, "that because you are, as you say, 'worried sick,' you are applying sick and irrational thoughts to your affairs and therefore making them go badly."

"Everything is washed up, finished," he moaned. "It's just all gone. Nothing left but a mess of worries. Nothing else at all."

"I'm sorry to hear that your wife has left you," I said sympathetically.

"Who said she has left me? My wife loves me and sticks to me loyally."

"That's great," I said. "Tell you what let's do. Suppose we compute what you have lost and what you have left. Let's first talk about what you have left," I suggested. "Then we will discuss what you have lost."

"We won't have anything to talk about in the first instance," he asserted darkly.

"Well, to start with you've got one pretty worthwhile asset. Your wife sticks with you and loves you." Then I added, "Too bad your children are no-account drug addicts and in jail."

"My children are not dope fiends! They are good kids—never been near a jail."

"Great! Then let's list that among your assets: 'Children not in jail.'" Then I continued, "It's tough about your house burning down with your insurance lapsed because of no money to pay the premium."

"Where did you get all that misinformation? My house hasn't burned down and I've got enough money to get by." By this time he had grasped the point of adding up blessings. "I'm a fool, a big fool," he admitted sheepishly. "I've never thought of the assets you mention."

We had a pleasant conversation and ended up praying together over the telephone.

He had a few bad times emotionally after this telephone interview, but he had given his thinking such a violent twist from negative to positive that the ultimate outcome was almost total victory over worry. He stopped worrying and really started living at age forty-five. And at any age this tremendous experience is just right for you, too.

Henry Ford: "Always Add Up the Best"

A writer friend of mine once interviewed Henry Ford, one of the great industrial geniuses of this country. Among other questions, he asked if worry had ever been a problem. Mr. Ford answered that it had somewhat until he had "become too busy to worry." He then gave the writer what he called a sure-fire formula for eliminating worry. And, as it was told to me, it went something like this— believe in the best, think your best, study your best, have a goal for your best, never be satisfied with less than your best, try your best, and in the long run things will turn out for the best. His concluding advice was, "Always add up the best."

FIVE WAYS TO CHECK YOUR WORRY HABIT

1. *Carefully practice listening to yourself.* Note and study with meticulous attention every comment you make, so you might become fully conscious of the amazing number of doleful and negative remarks you utter.

2. *Start being absolutely honest.* When you hear yourself making a negative statement, ask yourself: "Now look, do I honestly believe what I am saying or am I actually mouthing negativisms that I do not really believe at all?"

3. *Adopt the practice of saying exactly the opposite of what you usually say and note how much better the new affirmations sound.* As you continue this new procedure, it will become even more exciting to hear words and ideas full of life, hope, and expectancy coming from your mouth instead of the old defeatist remarks.

4. *Keep track of everything that happens as you work this new procedure.* Carefully note and compute even the smallest results. If you have been, for example, in the habit of saying glumly, "Things aren't going to go well today," now note how well things are going.

5. *Practice putting the best construction on every person and action each day.* This is one of the most exciting of all personal development practices. I first came upon it through the late Harry Bullis, a leading figure in the flour-milling industry in Minneapolis. Harry was a genuinely enthusiastic man, so much so that I asked for an explanation of his happy nature. "I decided long ago," he said, "to put the best possible connotation on the words and actions of every person and every situation. Naturally I was not blind to the realities, but I always tried first to emphasize the best connotation, for I believe that such practice actually helps stimulate a good out-

come. This best connotation practice resulted in enthusiasm for people, for business, for church, and other interests, and greatly helped me toward a worry-free life."

Confident: I Can Change for the Better

Most of us will admit that some things need changing in our lives. Discordant elements in personality often contribute to failure and unhappiness. We may possess traits that turn people off and interfere with good personal relationships. Perhaps certain weaknesses and inadequacies plague us. Under such circumstances you will welcome the good news that power is available to change your life.

This amazing power is the life of God in you. It is a vast force which, when focused, produces spectacular changes in personality.

THE POWER SOURCE

A man drove to my farm home in the country. He was accompanied by his wife. They were gifted people, nonchurchgoing. He was a publisher, she a writer—both extraordinarily capable. He said, "Helen and I are unhappy and frustrated. Neither of us is really well physically. Life has gone stale. Actually, we've hit a dead end. We need help." He went on to

49

explain that each to a degree had lost the creative touch. They just didn't seem to have it anymore. And then he added, "We do not want to remain as we are. We want this change you are always talking about. How do we get it?"

Knowing them to be what you might call sophisticated people, I wondered whether they could accept the basic simplicity of contacting the power they were asking for. So I said, "You are dissatisfied with yourselves as you are, is that correct? Just how dissatisfied are you?"

"Completely," they replied.

"And do I understand that you want to be changed and changed now?" The answer was affirmative.

Then I asked, "Are you willing now to separate from your life everything contrary to the spirit of Christ? And I mean everything!"

After some discussion as to what this entailed, it was evident that they were so desirous of the power to change their lives that they would go the whole distance.

We then went into a process of spiritual catharsis, which involved an honest emptying out of wrong attitudes, such as resentments, hostilities, and other mental festers. It was obvious they meant business. They weren't fooling.

"Now," I continued, "no human being can give you the power to change your life. Only Christ can do that. Therefore, are you now willing to commit yourselves to Christ, accepting him as your Savior and the renewer of life?"

Each offered a humble and obviously sincere prayer of self-commitment. Always when awareness of need joins with complete sincerity the power is given. They wanted it, they asked for it, they received it.

The change in them over succeeding months was remarkable. Life took on new meaning, deeper joy, greater satisfaction.

They came back the next spring seeming vital and in perfect health. They were excited about everything. Helen was almost ecstatic. "Never have I seen such a spring. The skies are bluer, the sunshine more golden, the songs of the birds are sweeter."

They began applying their talents to inspirational writing. They became active in helping others to find the same wonderful new power they had discovered.

YOU CAN HAVE A HAPPY FAMILY LIFE

The family unit—husband and wife, children, in-laws, grandparents—has an enormous potential for happiness or unhappiness, for love or for misunderstanding and conflict.

When a family lives together in affection and mutual respect, it results in probably the happiest state of life on earth. But when the family is disrupted by misunderstanding and conflict it creates an unhealthy state, one of continuing adverse effect in the lives of all, especially children.

10 Steps to a Changed Life

1. Realize that the power to change your life comes through faith in Christ.
2. Give yourself and all your problems to God.
3. Practice the relaxed faith principle—"Let go and let God."
4. Ask God for the power to live a new life. Believe he will supply it.
5. Go through the New Testament making a list of the actual words of Jesus and commit them to memory.
6. Ask yourself what Jesus would do. Then try doing that.
7. Form habits of daily prayer. Set aside specific times for prayer and give them top priority.
8. Read the New Testament from begining to end, stopping to study passages that particularly appeal to you.
9. Saturate your consciousness with Christ-centered thoughts.
10. Practice love and good will for people.

Reasonable, intelligent, sincere human beings of any age can, if they will, live together in peace and, indeed, in joyful relationship. If such a condition does not prevail in your family, this is to remind you that you definitely have the power to change your life within the family.

What steps may be taken to bring about a

happy family relationship?

1. *Let it begin with you.* Determine that you will begin to create within yourself the upbeat spirit that can rejuvenate the family life.

2. *Ask yourself this question:* "Am I personally contributing to family happiness or unhappiness?" Be sure you answer that question with absolute honesty.

3. *Correct within yourself any mistrust or hostility* and practice treating everyone in the family not only with love, but with respect for their opinions. Give them genuine esteem.

4. *Consider yourself a love "cell" and act lovingly.* Do not tell the family you have decided to be this new way. Just be it. They will pick it up. The new spirit injected by you will have effect.

Let me tell you about a young man in his late teens, definitely of the "now" generation—rebellious and contemptuous of every generation but his own. His parents got their backs up, the generation gap grew wider, the family drifted apart and the household was in a state of unhappiness.

Then this boy had a deep spiritual experience with Jesus Christ. As a result, he decided that instead of being part of the world's problems he would be part of its cure. Still sticking to his own views but now respecting others' opinions as well, he started practicing love in the family. He became a pleasant and lovable person within himself. Results? The family got together on a deeper level. He stimulated change in the others. The family became a unit wherein everybody loved and respected each other.

5. *Encourage every other family member, young and old, to hold each other in esteem as persons.* Everyone should accept each other and let everyone be himself. Identity of personality must always be respected. Love within the family will create a climate of goodwill and—what is equally important—real understanding.

6. *Be realistic.* Do not expect that everyone is going to change at once, or that change will necessarily come easily. There may be the resistance of long-held resentments, and even prejudice, that will be reduced only by a gradual process. The principal factor is that someone must start the change and let it pick up momentum from there.

7. *Develop a profound faith and reliance upon God* for guidance within the home and in all the family connections. When the Bible says, "Except the Lord build the house, they labor in vain that build it" (Ps. 127:1), it is a reminder of a time-tested truth that the family with religious faith tends to overcome problems and meet situations, while families without it often fail.

8. *Begin a program of definite, earnest prayer for each family member.* One person doing this regular type of praying, though he may not mention it to the others, will in time unconsciously motivate others to a new, spiritually-oriented attitude. When prayer be-

54

comes a group activity in the family, the members will grow together in a deeper fellowship. It is quite true that the family that prays together stay together.

A twenty-year-old girl was considerably upset in trying to find herself. Her attitude had been one of constant hostility, especially toward her father. But one night she had a confrontation with him: "Dad," she said, "you're really nice. In fact, you're a good guy. Tell me what you've been doing. Come on, come clean."

Her father then told her that he had been trying out a program of prayer that he would be able to change his own life and attitudes, be a better father, better husband, better member of the family. He hesitated and then said softly, "I pray for everyone, especially you; for in my heart I guess I've always had a special feeling for you, despite our conflicts."

"I knew you had been up to something," she said, and for the first time in weeks gave him a kind of love pat. In the following days this father and daughter drew together. And in time their secret leaked out. Ultimately it changed the entire family. They proved the power to change life in the family.

YOU CAN ENJOY YOUR JOB
If a person wants to change his life, perhaps he will have to change his job.

There are two ways to change jobs. The obvious one is to leave the job you now have and take another one. But if you do this it is usually assumed that all the things you dislike about the present job will be absent in the new job and that, indeed, everything in the new job will be just fine. And that, of course, isn't necessarily so.

There is a law of human nature that has to be reckoned with: You take yourself wherever you go. You can never get away from yourself. So, when you go from an unhappy job to a new job, you will, in the very nature of the case, take yourself along. This means, obviously, that the same weaknesses and wrong attitudes that you had in the old position will, after the first flush of enthusiasm, be there with you the same as ever. So the second way to change jobs is to change yourself. And that can be done within the framework of the present job.

A man consulted me about his job. He said it held no opportunity. It was a dead end. He was going to chuck it and go to something else. I outlined the above concept of dealing with a job. Then I mentioned the name of a dynamic man who was very successful. "What do you think Mr. Smith would do with your present job if he had it?"

He thought a minute and then said, "Well, I'm sure he would make it a success; he always makes everything succeed."

"Yes, but how would he succeed with this job?" I persisted. "What would he do?"

To which he replied, "I just don't know what he would do."

"Well, why not spend a few days trying to think what the highly successful Mr. Smith would do in this job and then you do that."

Later he returned with quite an improved attitude. He said, "The only way I can do what Mr. Smith would do is to become an outgoing person like Mr. Smith is. He is a positive thinker. Guess I'd better start practicing positive thinking, too." Encouraged, he followed his new mental attitude and did a rather creative job on himself. His job performance improved. He got a new job by changing himself in his present job.

YOU CAN THROW AWAY YOUR PERSONALITY CRUTCHES

Some people, being insecure, depend upon crutches to prop up a faltering personality. Faced with a deep inner conflicted feeling of inadequacy and believing they are unable to cope with problems, they go for crutches: drugs, for example, or alcohol or compulsive eating. Or in less dramatic ways they try to compensate for a miserable feeling of inferiority. What such persons really want is the power to change their lives.

One of the specialties of Jesus Christ is the elimination of crutches. Remember the man by the Pool of Bethesda? There was a legend that whenever an angel stirred the water whoever first got in would be healed.

This man had been lying by the pool for years until he had achieved a kind of status among the lame, the halt, and the blind.

This position served as a crutch for his mixed-up personality. He made the excuse that he could never get into the water first. The fact was that he did not want to be healed, for then he would have had to face life.

But Jesus, who knows the inner working of the human mind, bored straight into his consciousness. "Do you really want to be healed?" he demanded. The man squirmed under his direct gaze but then felt hope for the first time. He answered a firm, "Yes, I do want to be healed." Jesus instructed him to get to his feet, throw away his crutch, and really live.

A crutch very widely used today is alcohol. I met a man at a reception who had had several cocktails and definitely showed the effects. "Why do I do this?" he asked. "Actually I don't really like it. But I have a shy streak in me and am tongue-tied in conversation. A few cocktails loosen me up, turning me from an introvert to an extrovert. I am just no good socially without the lift alcohol gives me."

My guess is that there are many who drink for this reason. In effect, they are leaning on a crutch. To be a good conversationalist who really communicates, all you have to do is be up on things. You don't need to hobble around on an alcohol crutch.

The pity is that this kind of dependence can and often does turn into alcoholism, one of the most acute forms of defeat. The alcoholic is truly a crippled personality.

Such a person can be cured, however. One of the most important agencies in this process is Alcoholics Anonymous, whose record of giving people the power to change their lives is phenomenal. We have seen many astonishing recoveries through the power of God. This power is always available, but the alcoholic must come to the point where he depends upon God absolutely, having no reserve dependence upon himself.

So, in the name of Jesus, throw away your crutch and enjoy life at its best.

Expectant: I Have a Future!

THE BEST GUIDE TO THE FUTURE

You've got a future! Despite the way you may feel about your prospects and all that you are told by the purveyors of bad news, you've really got a future.

No matter how tough things may be, or how hard the going, or how discouraged you are, you've got a future.

Regardless of how old, or tired, or sick you feel, still you've got a future. However unjustly you think you have been treated by life and by circumstances, remember, always remember, *you've got a future!*

The future is a big business today. It seems that many people are going all out for astrology and horoscopes. Astrology is said to have originated in Chaldea and around the Persian Gulf. Kings of Chaldea and Babylon had staff astrologers to advise them concerning the future. The pharaohs of Egypt also used astrology.

Today it seems astrologers are back in

business. Out of 1,750 daily newspapers in the United States, 1,220 carry an astrology column and print horoscopes. People are concerned about the future, thus the interest in horoscopes.

In a large bookstore, I noticed three tables of books on astrology and occult science. Only one table was required for religious books. Apparently, when the future seems uncertain many people turn to bizarre, even magical sources for comfort and presumed guidance.

This chapter, however, is designed to remind you that Jesus Christ has the answer to your future, your country's future, the world's future. The wise course is to put yourself in his hands, for he knows all about the future, all about your future. This is the secret of having a great future.

How then does one realize his or her future? First, by developing a pattern of thought that is built around an optimistic concept of the future. *Think* future; *talk* future; *believe* future; *act* future. Live on the basis that the old is in the past, the new is here and yet to be.

WHEN THE FUTURE BOTTOMS OUT

It is really very sad how people having difficulty or illness or discouragement tend to discount their future. For example, when my wife and I were in Italy not long ago, we met such a person. It came about this way. Mrs. Peale announced she wanted to buy a Pucci dress. "What is a Pucci dress?" I inquired. "I have never heard of it."

"A Pucci dress," she informed me, "is a dress made by a designer named Pucci from Florence. They're very distinctive, and he signs every dress."

"Anything that's signed is going to cost money," I said jokingly.

"But I can buy this dress here for a lot less than in New York," she told me.

"Well," I said, giving in, "I'm glad we're going to save some money on it, anyway!"

While I was sitting in the reception room, a man came in, reluctantly, it appeared. He was a big fellow with a little wife, but you could see who really was in charge. He nodded to me and asked, "Are you an American?"

"Yes," I replied, "I am. Are you?"

"Yes," and then, confidentially, "Did your wife drag you into this place?"

"Well," I admitted, "I guess she did." He asked me what I was doing. "Oh, traveling around, making a speech or two, having a little vacation. What are you doing?" I asked.

"I've been to Ischia," he said. "Been there for three weeks taking those baths."

"I'm sure they did you good," I commented.

"I don't know. I was told I wouldn't feel any different for six months. But," he sighed, "to tell you the truth, I haven't got a whole lot of confidence in them anyway. I'm getting old, you know, and you can't do much about that. Let's face it, I haven't got a future."

"My friend," I said, "you mustn't talk that

way. You must say to yourself, 'I know that those baths are going to help me tremendously.' You must say, 'I'm not an old man. I am filled with vigor and health, and I'm going to live creatively.' You mustn't think the way you've been talking."

After listening to my suggestions, he said, "You know something? You sound like a fellow back in the United States who once wrote a book on positive thinking." When I told him he was talking to that same man, he could hardly believe me!

Don't go through life saying, "I don't feel good." "I'm tired." "I've lost my enthusiasm." "I'm getting old." "I don't amount to anything." "I have no future." That kind of talk, which comes from the wrong kind of thinking, is a sure way to guarantee no future. Instead, affirm, "I'm happy, I'm enthusiastic. With God, I have a future."

HE FOUND HIS FUTURE

Let me share with you a letter from a man in Pennsylvania.

No words that I may now write or ever speak can convey that amount of gratitude I feel for you. You have completely changed my life by giving me the chance to understand the love of Christ.

More than three years ago I dropped out of college. I had barely a "C" average and felt that college had nothing to interest me. Well, anyway, I dropped out and got married to a sweet and wonderful woman. Although the only job I could find was in a gas station, she was behind me 100 percent. Although I made some progress and made a good income, I always felt that something was missing.

Then one day after the birth of my son and daughter I realized that I had no future. And that's an awful thing to feel. I knew that to advance with the oil company I worked for I would have to return to college, but fear of failure and insecurity held me back.

Then that glorious day came one year ago when I bought a book of yours and my life began to change. The book showed me a Jesus I had never known, a Jesus that is willing to help you. I began to pray, not only for myself, but for other people as well. I began talking to Jesus. I began to feel confidence and peace for the first time in months. My friends noticed the difference, and even those people I dislike responded to my prayers and we began to build friendships we had never known before.

Your book, *The Power of Positive Thinking,* gave me the courage to enroll in college once again. But my schedule was a difficult one, for I continued in my regular job forty-five hours a week in the evenings while attending college full-time during the day. Everything worked out better than I ever could have imagined. My family and myself were never happier; my performance at my job improved tremendously. And I was elected to the Dean's list at school with a 4.0 or straight "A" average.

But I must say that the credit is mine only in a small way. The credit rightly goes to you and to our Lord. You taught me how to find God's power for my life. And I devised a system whereby I had time every day to talk to Jesus.

I travel thirty miles every day to school and work. I used to leave the house at the last minute, but at the suggestion of a friend I started the process of leaving one-half hour early and stopping at a small dairy mart for what I now call a cup of coffee and a cup of Jesus. For twenty minutes I sit in my truck, relax, sip my coffee, and pray.

I could never have made it without Jesus, and I could never have understood Jesus without you. This is why no words can really express the warm love and gratitude that I feel. Now I know that I have a wonderful future!

Of course this man has a wonderful future. When he found Jesus, the gloom, negativism, discouragement, and frustration dropped from his mind; a new attitude took over. Then when he put his words into action by enrolling in school, his future became a mighty reality.

How I wish I could convince you, as you read this, that you may nullify, perhaps even destroy your future if you persist in thinking you have no future. But you can create a future if you really believe that you have one and then give the supervision of it to God.

Every day of your life when you wake up, say, "With God, I've got a future." That is what you are intended to have. You and I are meant to live life until the last, believing in a future and then going on to the eternal future. Tell yourself every day, "With God I've got a future so much greater than any future I ever had before."

FAITH ON THE EXPRESSWAY

Three people were in an automobile on an expressway in the Chicago area. Dayle Gruetzmacher and her husband, Amber, were in a station wagon with their daughter Sue. The traffic was heavy and the road slick from rain as Amber pulled to a halt behind a line of vehicles. As he looked in the rearview mirror, he saw the most terrifying sight in all of his years of driving. A huge trailer truck was sliding across the highway out of control, headed for his car.

One second later it spun the car around and then fell directly on top of it with crushing force. Shattering glass. Crunching metal. Fumes of gasoline. Silence.

The mother found herself with her knees wedged against her chest scarcely able to breathe. With difficulty, she could move her hands and head, but the crushed roof of the car was just a few inches above her head. Her husband was in a contortion, his trapped legs oddly twisted. One leg was bent under him, the other leg sticking out of the shattered window of the car and jammed against the side of the gigantic truck. Sue was flat on her back and could hardly move.

No one was in severe pain, no bones were broken, and no one was bleeding; but they could do nothing to help themselves. The capsized truck covered and surrounded their battered car. These three persons met this horrifying situation by thanking God that they were still alive. They had a tremendous sense that God was with them there in the wrecked car, which might yet become their coffin.

A friendly face appeared, a passing motorist, astonished to find anybody alive. He assured them that help was on the way. They continued to pray as the diesel fuel from the capsized truck mingled with the gasoline with their own gas tank. A single spark could ignite it all. Then they realized that the roof of the car was slowly settling down. Inch by inch the enormous weight of the truck was taking the last vestige of resistance out of the crumpled station wagon.

An hour passed; two hours. A fireman appeared with a tube connected to an oxygen supply and they were able to breathe more easily. Then what did they do? They actually began to sing hymns of faith. And they reassured one another, "God knows how much we can take."

Finally came the critical moment when a crane lifted the truck. If it should slip from the crane, their car would be completely crushed. To safeguard against that possibility the truck was shored up with beams, and three hours from the moment they were first incarcerated they were released from their prison. Taken to a hospital after their miraculous escape, they were quickly released. People asked, "How could you have such calmness?"

"We are in God's hands here in this world and we will be in his hands over there," was their reply. In effect they were saying, "Whatever happens, when we are in God's hands, we have a future."

Does the future have to do only with outcomes in this mortal life? Does the future have a boundary beyond which there is nothing? Not at all! The future is limitless, projecting far out into eternity itself. Time does not determine futures. Nor does age nor circumstances. If you have a future in Christ, that future is for always.

So again I say, "You've got a future!"

A Winner's Guide to Eleven Common Problems

HOW TO COPE WITH DIFFICULTY

1. Affirm. Affirm, and continue to affirm until you believe that with God's help you can cope with the difficulty.

2. No Panic. Let there be no panic, for a difficulty can never be handled emotionally. Always keep it cool.

3. Organize. Organize the difficulty. Take it apart and study its component elements. New insights will come to you.

4. Think. Always apply sound, reasonable thinking.

5. Why Me? Do not ask, "Why me?" or feel imposed upon when any difficulty comes. That is the way life is. Everybody has difficulty sooner or later.

6. Patience. Practice patience, for some difficulties are not handled overnight.

7. Acceptance. Acceptance is important. Tell God that if you have to live with this difficulty you will accept his will and know that he will give you the strength needed.

8. Learn. Look for the educational value in

a difficulty so that you can handle a like situation another time.

9. Bigger. Every day affirm: "God is bigger than anything that can happen to me."

10. Let Go and Let God. When you have done all you can do, put the difficulty in God's hands with confidence that he will show you the solution.

HOW TO OVERCOME WORRY

1. Habit. Such is worry, developed over a long period of time. And any habit that can be formed can also be broken. So the first step is to start breaking yourself of the worry habit.

2. Strangle. That is the basic meaning of the word *worry:* to strangle or choke. It can cut off your natural energy and effectiveness. Do not strangle yourself with worrisome thoughts.

3. Foolish. That is what worry is. A foolish waste of mental energy. It has been computed that 40 percent of your worries concern the past, 50 percent are related to the future, and 10 percent are about present problems. Ninety-two percent of most worries never happen. You can handle the remaining 8 percent.

4. Forget. An effective way to stop worrying about past mistakes is to become skilled in forgetting. The past is past, so forget it. Every day say aloud: "Forgetting those things which are behind, and reaching forth unto those things which are before, I press toward the mark for the prize of the high calling of God in Christ Jesus" (Phil. 3:13, 14).

5. *Overlook.* "The essence of genius is to know what to overlook," so said the great psychologist-philosopher William James. When the worrier learns to overlook, attention is lessened, uptightness disintegrates, and a new attitude can be "skip it." This is important to the healing of worry.

6. *Future.* Stop looking for dark spots in the future. Look for a future full of light, one in which God watches over you. Do not worry about what may happen, but create good happenings through faith.

7. *Imperturbable.* You will not be a worrier when you cultivate the attitude of imperturbability. Regardless of anxiety or stress, say and believe, "God is keeping me calm and peaceful."

8. *Empty.* The mind can be emptied of anything. So, if you have filled it with worry thoughts, start now to empty those thoughts out of your mind. One way to do this is to declare with authority: "I am now emptying my mind of all worry, anxiety, fear, insecurity."

9. *Fill.* The mind is so constituted that it will not long remain empty. It must be filled with something positive or the negative thought pattern of worry will return. So every day deliberately practice filling your mind with strong, healthy thoughts. Say aloud: "God is now filling my mind with courage, strength, peace, and assurance."

10. Presence. One of the greatest techniques for courageous living is the practice of the presence of God. Learn to know that God is with you every minute, day and night. Use this affirmation daily: "God will never leave me. I am never alone. His presence protects me."

HOW TO DEAL WITH LONELINESS

1. Resources. Look for unexplored resources within yourself. There are many which have not yet been discovered and which will make you more interesting to yourself.

2. Company. Have you ever thought of yourself as good company, someone you can enjoy being with? Many people find that they can have a good time with themselves.

3. Interesting. Fill your mind full of interesting thoughts, do interesting things, read interesting books, become interested in what goes on in the world.

4. Forget. The lonely person intensifies loneliness by becoming obsessed with himself or herself. One of life's greatest skills is that of forgetting one's self.

5. Fun. Be a fun sort of person. Laugh a good deal of the time. Develop an acute ability to see and appreciate the humorous side of everything. The more fun you are, the less lonely you are bound to be, for people like fun persons.

6. Plenty. A lonely life can be barren and therefore unhappy. The counteractive secret is in the word *plentiful*. Have plenty of activity, plenty of interests, plenty of new experiences. Fill your mind and your life full of plenty.

7. *Program*. Have a plan for every day. Do something interesting, something different. Go a lot of places, see a lot of things, try to get acquainted with many people.

8. *Look*. All around you everywhere are lonely people. Look for them and you will find them. Since you have been lonely yourself, you will be better able to recognize them.

9. *Do*. Try to relieve the loneliness of others. Nobody is going to stay lonely very long who does things for people. The more you do to make life less lonely and unhappy for individuals the less lonely and unhappy your life will become.

10. *Companionship*. Actually, no one ever needs to be alone. Even on a desert island in the midst of the sea, you are not alone— Someone is with you. Cultivate the companionship of the Great Friend.

HOW TO RELAX TENSION

1. *Uptight*. Do not permit yourself to be drawn up taut. Imagine yourself to be a tightly-drawn rubberband. Now let go and snap back to normal. In your thinking contrast *down-easy* with *uptight*.

2. *Minute*. Scatter one-minute quiet periods throughout the day. Just stand still for a moment. Spend a minute thinking about God.

Take one-minute looks at the hills or clouds. See how many such moments you can accumulate in a day.

3. Breathe. When you feel stress coming on, take a deep breath, then exhale. Do it again. Do it a third time. Deep breathing, in and out, tends to exhale tension.

4. Leaf. Sit for a moment in an easy chair. Put your head against the back, extend your feet. Raise your hands and allow them to fall limply on your knees like a wet leaf on a log. What is more relaxed than a wet leaf on a log?

5. Visualize. Take a moment to visualize the most peaceful and beautiful place you have ever been in your life. Return to it now by the magic of memory and savor once again the healing effect it had on you. Take a memory trip to some beautiful valley or sea beach or flower-stewn meadow.

6. Peace. Conceive of the peace of God that passes understanding now touching your mind and every part of your physical being. Feel it permeating deeply into your spirit. Affirm aloud: "The peace of God is changing my tension into relaxation."

7. Drain. Consciously and deliberately drain out of your mind every agitated, unnerving, tensed-up thought. See these thoughts as flowing out of your mental apparatus, out—out—out. Let them go, now.

8. Words. Practice the healing therapy of words. Not harsh and strident words, but mellifluous, melodic, peaceful words. Say them slowly, extracting from them their deepest essence. Say words such as *tranquility, serenity, quietness, restfulness.*

9. *Quiet.* A ten-minute quiet time everyday can be a powerful antidote to tension. In the quiet time read a poem, a passage of Scripture, pray, and meditate. If this procedure is repeated day after day, it will undermine tension.

10. *Repeat.* Daily and nightly repeat three times, aloud if possible, the following relaxing statements: "Thou wilt keep him in perfect peace, whose mind is stayed on thee" (Isa. 26:3); "Come unto me, all ye that labor and are heavy laden, and I will give you rest" (Matt. 11:28); and "Peace I give unto you: not as the world giveth, give I unto you. Let not your heart be troubled, neither let it be afraid" (John 14.27).

HOW TO MEET SORROW

1. *Philosophy.* To begin with, one must have a philosophical realization that there are certain inevitabilities in human experience which must come to each of us. Such philosophy will prepare you for sorrow and help you meet it when it comes.

2. *Goodness.* Nothing that God ever ordained is bad. Therefore, God's goodness is to be found even in our sorrows. His goodness is given to your loved one who has gone and it is given to you who remain.

3. *Continue.* For your own normal readjustment, continue your life of activities as before. Don't avoid places that were familiar

to your loved one. Carry on as before; in due time, the knowledge that your loved one would want you to do so will comfort you.

4. *Lose.* Never say you have "lost" your wife, husband, child, brother, or sister. Remember the words of the poet: "Love can never lose its own." You have not lost that loved one, they are merely living in a new dimension and are not very far away.

5. *House.* "Where is my loved one?" the sorrowing heart asks. And the answer is a simple one. Your loved one is in the Father's house of many mansions, surrounded by love and beauty, and is well, strong, and happy. Just tell yourself he or she is all right—quite all right.

6. *Meet.* Remember the old hymn, "In the sweet bye-and-bye, we shall meet on that beautiful shore." Hold to that as a fact, as the truth. God made it possible for us to meet here, and he also will make it possible for us to meet "over there."

7. *Heal.* Perhaps the best way to heal your own sorrow is to help heal someone else's grief. When you give out sympathy and love, they come back to you doubled. Make a list of all the sad people you know, and try to bring comfort to them. You will find amazing comfort and healing for yourself in doing so.

8. *Absorb.* Know one great fact about yourself: With God, you can absorb any experience, however sorrowful, and come up victorious. There is an adjustable and resilient mechanism in human nature, and when a

person has a deep religious faith the recovery from grief comes easier.

9. Expression. Give normal expression to your grief. Do not try to bottle it up and contain it. God made tears for a purpose, and that was to relieve. A tear is agony in solution. Don't be ashamed of your grief or try to repress it. Cry it out and pray it out, and peace will come.

10. Resurrection. Perhaps the greatest healing of sorrow is to be found in your faith. Repeat some of the great words of Jesus, who understands your sorrow. Use such statements as, "Jesus said, 'I am the resurrection and the life. He that believeth in me, though he were dead, yet shall he live . . . Whosoever liveth and believeth in me shall never die' " (John 11:25, 26).

HOW TO CURE AN INFERIORITY COMPLEX

1. Competent. Form a mental picture of yourself as being a compentent, effective, and successful person. Hold that image firmly in mind and do not let any self-doubt erase it. Presently your mental processes will go to work to actualize this image of yourself.

2. Cancel. Whenever a negative thought about yourself and your qualifications comes to mind, immediately cancel it out as unworthy, untrue, and unrealistic. The more vigorously you cancel it out, the weaker it will become, until it will disappear altogether.

3. Obstacles. Never build up an obstacle of any kind in your mind. See an obstacle realistically, then affirm that—with God's help—you can handle it successfully.

4. Awed. Don't ever be awed by any other person or group of persons. Never copy anyone else. There is only one you, and that makes you special. So have respect for yourself as you are and regard others fearlessly.

5. Ten. Ten powerful words emphasized and believed can cure all inferiority and inadequacy feeling. Repeat these ten words at least ten times every day—aloud preferably. Say them as you go to sleep so that they may seep into the unconscious. Here are the words: "If God be for us, who can be against us?" (Rom. 8:31). Substitute "me" for "us."

6. Understand. When you understand the reasons for your inferiority feelings, you are on your way to victory over them. To know and to understand is the beginning of healing. Inferiority feelings usually begin in childhood and often become overlaid with mystery. This creates a tendency to accept them as final. But they are not natural, they are acquired. Understand them, and be free.

7. Strengthen. The victim of inferiority feels weak and ineffective. He isn't, really. But thinking so means he must be built up in strength. Repetition of the following words will enhance strength: "I can do all things through Christ which strengtheneth me" (Phil. 4:13).

8. Estimate. Thoughtfully and realistically,

with complete honesty, estimate your abilities. Then, to compensate for negative underevaluation, raise the estimate 10 percent. Don't worry about becoming egotistical. Work to develop a wholesome, normal self-respect.

9. Spiritual. The person who suffers from inferiority is low in spiritual vitality. Increasing the spiritual content in your thinking will normalize you as a child of God. Affirmative prayer—in which you give thanks to God for the enhanced spiritual force now operating within you—is effective.

10. Partnership. Realize that you are not facing life alone but that you have a partner, a great senior Partner, who always stands by to guide and help you. How can anything defeat that great partnership of God and yourself? With God, you will be equal to every demand made upon you.

HOW TO GET RID OF FEAR
1. Seek. Perhaps the most basic method for getting rid of fear is written in Psalm 34:4: "I sought the Lord, and he heard me, and delivered me from all my fears." Note the inclusive stress: *all.*

2. Trust. The opposite of fear is trust, so practice trust. Put your trust in God and in the fact that most of the things that you fear will never come to pass.

3. Rely. Rely on the law of averages that you will have safety. Rely on the mechanism you must use, such as buses, airplanes, or ships. Believe that you can trust efficiency, and rely on God.

4. Study. Study to discover the origin of your fears. There are reasons for your fear. And, since fear is highly conditioned emotionally, you may find that many of these reasons are irrational.

5. Add. Frequently try the technique of adding up all the times in your life when you know you have been taken care of, watched over, and protected. Follow this by the affirmation that it always will be that way.

6. Do. Emerson's advice is sound: "Do the thing you fear, and the death of fear is certain." If you are afraid to do something, yet doing that something makes sense, do it. As you act, your fear will subside.

7. Courage. Mentally and spiritually emphasize courage. This will start the process of canceling out fear thoughts. Think courageously, act courageously, and fear will yield to courage.

8. See. Form an image of yourself as now being free of all fear. What we deeply picture tends, finally, to be actualized as fact.

9. Help. Do a good turn for someone else who is fearful by helping that individual to overcome his own fears. In helping another to lose a fear, the hold of your own fear will be lessened.

10. Faith. The second most powerful force in the world is fear. But the most powerful force of all is faith. Faith is stronger than fear. So, to get rid of fear, build up your faith.

HOW TO HAVE A SUCCESSFUL MARRIAGE

1. Emotion. The first rule in a successful marriage is to be sure that you are grown up emotionally. Marriage is for the mature, not the infantile. The fusion of two different personalities requires emotional balance and control on the part of each.

2. Cornerstone. Every kind of building requires a cornerstone. This is no less true of building a marriage. And the required and important cornerstone of any marriage is expressed in the following words: "Except the Lord build the house, they labour in vain that build it" (Ps. 127:1).

3. Argument. Talk out all your problems together and arrive at reasonable solutions in unity. A good discussion, even a controlled argument, is OK. But be sure to keep it devoid of emotion. Decide everything not on *who* is right, but on *what* is right.

4. Best. A happy marriage will always result when each partner tries to bring out the best in the other. Two people loving each other with high esteem for the other's personality are bound to get along beautifully.

5. Polite. Plain courtesy is an asset in marriage. Be polite and courteous to each other. Never let anger make you discourteous. The human personality responds to esteem. Respect each other.

6. Mutual. It is important to remember that marriage is a relationship based on mutual responsibility. Both persons must share equally in the partnership. Certainly, neither should dominate the other.

7. Adjustment. A good marriage depends upon adjustment. This adjustment must be achieved on all levels: physical, emotional, mental, and spiritual. And the adjusting must be done by each party.

8. Team. Live, play, and work as a team in which each partner makes an equal contribution to the total effort of the marriage. Do things together often, and develop an interest in what the other is doing. Make all decisions on a team basis.

9. Night. Pray together before going to sleep every night. Pray together about all decisions and about all problems. The couple who prays together will grow together, stick together, and win victories together.

10. Exciting. Make it an exciting experience to do for the other every kindly, loving thing you can think of. If each one tries to make the other happy, both will be happy and the marriage will be a successful one.

HOW TO SOLVE A PROBLEM

1. Seeds. The way to start out in solving a problem is to entertain a solid belief that for every problem there is a solution. Indeed, every problem contains the seeds of its own solution. You can find the answer to your problem if you look deeply into the problem itself.

2. Calm. A basic premise for solving a problem is to remain emotionally calm. Uptightness can block off the flow of thought power. Therefore it is important to reduce the stress and tension elements, for the mind can only operate efficiently when the emotions are under control.

3. *Assemble.* In dealing with a problem a proper procedure is to assemble all of the facts impartially, impersonally, and judicially. Take a scientific attitude toward the elements of the problem.

4. *Paper.* Lay out all of the component parts of the problem on paper, so that you can see them in orderly coherence. Such a procedure will help clarify your thinking by bringing the various factors of a problem into systematic order. When you can see clearly, you will be better able to think clearly.

5. *Force.* Never try to force an answer to a problem. Keep your mind relaxed and allow the solution to open up naturally and become clear. The danger in trying to force an answer is that you may be forcing what you want rather than what is right.

6. *Prayer.* Subject your problem to intensive prayer. Believe and affirm that through divine guidance you will receive insights and mental illumination. Spiritual understanding inevitably produces the best possible solution.

7. *Counsel.* Often we need help with a problem. It is valuable, therefore, to get wise counsel. Employ, then, the thought contained in Psalm 73:24: "Thou shalt guide me with thy counsel." Such high-level counsel is replete with wisdom.

8. *Intuition.* There is a subtle quality of mental processes which may be described as

intuition, or the feel and impression of the right thing to do. This intuitive procedure is best conditioned by prayer and spiritual insight in which you try to think God's thoughts about the problem.

9. Meditate. Let the problem free-float in your mind. Refrain from pressure, tension, or even timing. Simply allow it to subsist in unhurried mental activity. The mind will therefore produce the answer when needed.

10. Creative. Put your trust in the creative power of your mind to arrive at a proper answer through the process of thinking, praying, and affirming. Let God guide you through the method of insight to come up with a solution to your problem.

HOW TO GET ALONG WITH PEOPLE

1. Like. If you genuinely like people, like to be with them, like to talk with them, and like to be helpful to them, you will find that people generally will like you. When mutual liking exists, people get along with one another.

2. Interest. Always be interested in the other person's activities and ideas. Direct conversation to the other's interests rather than talking about yourself. If you are absorbed in another's interests, he will become attentive to yours and you will have a pleasant time together.

3. Likable. To be liked and to get along with others it's necessary to be a likable person. Practice the old saying, "To have friends, be friendly."

4. Names. Practice the art of remembering names. To accomplish this, give attention to the other person so that his name will register. Realize that a person's name is important to him, so remembering names will help you get along.

5. Easy. Be easy to get along with. Be a comfortable sort of person, so that there is no strain in being with you. Be an "old shoe" kind of individual. Be homey, down-to-earth.

6. Stimulating. Cultivate the quality of being stimulating. If being with you makes people feel better and more alive, you will be sought after and your personal relations will be excellent.

7. Scratchy. Personal relations deteriorate when a person has scratchy elements in the personality. That is to say, do not rub people the wrong way. Be relaxed and affable.

8. Sensitive. Avoid being on edge and sensitive so that you are easily hurt. People instinctively shy away from the super-sensitive for fear of arousing an unpleasant reaction. Avoid the temptation to react with hurt feelings, and you will get along with people.

9. Heal. Sincerely attempt to heal on an honest basis every misunderstanding that you may have with others. Mentally and spiritually drain off your grievances and maintain an attitude of good will with everyone.

10. Do. Love people and do things for them. Perform unselfish and outgoing acts of friendship. Such sincere self-giving inevitably leads to pleasant personal relations. It is all summed up in a familiar Scripture admonition: "Do for others what you want them to do for you" (Matt. 7:12, TLB).

HOW TO TURN FAILURE INTO SUCCESS

1. Failure. Hold the thought that no failure is permanent, but that it is only a temporary setback in a successful life. Failure is an incident that can be woven into the tapestry of creative achievement. Remember, failure is only temporary.

2. Wrong. Failure may be defined as the wrong way to do something. Therefore, failure has advantageous elements in that it tells us how not to proceed. And when you know how something should not be done, you are in a better position to learn how it *should* be done.

3. Learn. While you may learn from your failures by discovering how not to proceed, you may learn more effectively from your successes by discovering how to proceed rightly.

4. Never. Never accept failure. Keep the failure context out of your thoughts. Infuse your mind with success concepts.

5. Think. Remember the sign Thomas A. Edison had on his office wall: "There is a better way to do it; find it." And how do you find it? By prayer-motivated discipline and creative thinking.

6. Diligence. No success can be attained in this life without diligence. Work and more work, diligently applied, is the "open sesame" to successful achievement. The ability to do the laborious tasks and keep on doing them is essential to successful outcomes.

7. Goal. All successful people have a goal. Not a fuzzy, indefinite objective, but a sharp, clearly-defined, specific goal. No one can get anywhere unless he knows where he wants to go and what he wants to be or do. Have a definite, prayer-oriented goal.

8. Right. Be sure that your goal is a right one, for nothing that is wrong will ever turn out to be right. Wrongness results in wrongness. Only rightness produces rightness, so be right.

9. Ask. To be certain you are doing what you ought to be doing with your life, ask God for direction. In the last analysis, only the God-directed life can attain true and basic success.

10. Way. The sure way to success is the way of unselfish prayer. Adopt the thought that you want to do the most good in the world, and achieve the best values—not just for yourself but for *all* people—and you will bring your total experience into the area of successful motivation.

About the Author

DR. NORMAN VINCENT PEALE was for
many years the minister of Marble Collegiate
Church in New York. He and his wife, Ruth
Stafford Peale, are copublishers of the inspi-
rational monthly magazine *Guideposts.* Dr.
Peale is the author of more than twenty
books, including *The Power of Positive
Thinking* (Revell) and *The Positive Power of
Jesus Christ* (Tyndale). The Peales live in
New York.

POCKET GUIDES
FROM TYNDALE

The Best Way to Plan Your Day by Edward Dayton and Ted Engstrom. With the guidelines in this book, you can learn to effectively set goals, determine priorities, and beat the time crunch. 72-0373-1

Christianity: Hoax or History? by Josh McDowell. Was Jesus Christ a liar, a lunatic, or Lord? A popular speaker and author looks at the resurrection of Jesus and other claims of the Christian faith. 72-0367-7

Demons, Witches, and the Occult by Josh McDowell and Don Stewart. Why are people fascinated with the occult? This informative guide will answer your questions about occult practices and their dangers. 72-0541-6

Family Budgets That Work by Larry Burkett. Customize a budget for your household with the help of this hands-on workbook. By the host of the radio talk show "How to Manage Your Money." 72-0829-6

Getting Out of Debt by Howard L. Dayton, Jr. At last, a no-nonsense approach to your money problems. Here's advice on creating a budget, cutting corners, making investments, and paying off loans. 72-1004-5

Make Your Dream Come True by Charles Swindoll. These ten inspirational chapters will lead any man or woman in the quest for inner strength and growth and help develop great character traits. 72-7007-2

Preparing for Childbirth by Debra Evans. Expectant moms can replace their fears about childbirth with joyful anticipation. Includes suggestions that will benefit both mothers and fathers. 72-4917-0

Raising Teenagers Right by James Dobson. Dr. Dobson, an authority on child development, answers some of the most-asked questions about the teenage years: how to implement discipline, build confidence, and discuss puberty. 72-5139-6